DISCOVER DOGS WITH THE AMERICAN CANINE ASSOCIATION

I LIKE SCHNAUZERS!

Linda Bozzo

It is the mission of the American Canine Association (ACA) to provide registered dog owners with the educational support needed for raising, training, showing, and breeding the healthiest pets expected by responsible pet owners throughout the world. Through our activities and services, we encourage and support the dog world in order to promote best-known husbandry standards as well as to ensure that the voice and needs of our customers are quickly and properly addressed.

Our continued support, commitment, and direction are guided by our customers, including veterinary, legal, and legislative advisors. ACA aims to provide the most efficient, cooperative, and courteous service to our customers and strives to set the standard for education and problem solving for all who depend on our services.

For more information, please visit www.acacanines.com, email customerservice@acadogs.com, phone 1-800-651-8332, or write to the American Canine Association at PO Box 121107, Clermont, FL 34712.

Published in 2019 by Enslow Publishing, LLC.
101 W. 23rd Street, Suite 240, New York, NY 10011

Library of Congress Cataloging-in-Publication Data

Names: Bozzo, Linda, author.
Title: I like schnauzers! / Linda Bozzo.
Description: New York : Enslow Publishing, 2019. | Series: Discover dogs with the American Canine Association | Audience: K to Grade 3. | Includes bibliographical references and index.
Identifiers: LCCN 2018010796| ISBN 9781978501935 (library bound) | ISBN 9781978502680 (paperback) | ISBN 9781978502697 (6 pack)
Subjects: LCSH: Schnauzers—Juvenile literature.
Classification: LCC SF429.S37 B69 2019 | DDC 636.73—dc23
LC record available at https://lccn.loc.gov/2018010796

Printed in the United States of America

To Our Readers: We have done our best to make sure all websites in this book were active and appropriate when we went to press. However, the author and the publisher have no control over and assume no liability for the material available on those websites or on any websites they may link to. Any comments or suggestions can be sent by email to customerservice@enslow.com.

Photo Credits: Cover, p. 1 Elayne Massaini/Shutterstock.com; p. 3 (left) otsphoto/Shutterstock.com; p. 3 (right) MGovantes/Shutterstock.com; p. 5 Dora Zett/Shutterstock.com; p. 6 MaraZe/Shutterstock.com; p. 9 BaileyOne/Shutterstock.com; p. 10 Tijana Stepic/EyeEm/Getty Images; p. 13 (left) cynoclub/Shutterstock.com; p 13 (right) graphicphoto/Thinkstock/(collar), Luisa Leal Photography/Shutterstock.com (bed), gvictoria/Shutterstock.com (brush), exopixel/Shutterstock.com (dishes), © iStockphoto.com/Lisa Thornberg (leash, toys); p. 14 beeboys/Shutterstock.com; p. 17 Steve Hoskins/The Image Bank/Getty Images; p. 18 135pixels/Shutterstock.com; p. 19 NataSnow/Shutterstock.com; p. 21 Zanna Pesnina/Shutterstock.com.

Enslow Publishing
101 W. 23rd Street
Suite 240
New York, NY 10011
USA
enslow.com

CONTENTS

IS A SCHNAUZER RIGHT FOR YOU?

Schnauzers are great family dogs and are good with children. This friendly breed can live just about anywhere.

There are three schnauzer breeds: standard, miniature, and giant!

A DOG OR A PUPPY?

Schnauzers are great learners, which makes them easy to train. If you do not have time to train a puppy, you may want an older schnauzer instead.

If not trained properly, a schnauzer can rule your household.

LOVING YOUR SCHNAUZER

Schnauzers are fun-loving and loyal and want a lot of attention. Love your schnauzer by spending lots of family time with him.

Schnauzers do well in agility competitions.

EXERCISE

Your schnauzer will enjoy playing games such as fetch with the family. To keep your schnauzer busy, take her for a walk on a leash or let her roam the yard.

Schnauzers have lots of energy!

FEEDING YOUR SCHNAUZER

Schnauzers can be fed wet or dry dog food. Ask a veterinarian (vet), a doctor for animals, which food is best for your dog and how much to feed her.

Give your schnauzer fresh, clean water every day.

Remember to keep your dog's food and water dishes clean. Dirty dishes can make a dog sick.

Do not feed your dog people food. It can make her sick.

Your new dog will need:

a collar with a tag

a bed

a brush

food and water dishes

a leash

toys

GROOMING

Schnauzers shed. This means their hair falls out, but schnauzers don't shed a lot. They can be bathed when needed. Make sure you use shampoo made specially for dogs.

Your schnauzer's nails will need to be clipped. A vet or groomer can show you how. Your dog's ears should be cleaned, and his teeth should be brushed by an adult.

Regular trimming is needed by a professional groomer.

WHAT YOU SHOULD KNOW

Miniature schnauzers were bred to hunt rats. They should not be trusted with small furry pets, such as hamsters and guinea pigs.

Schnauzers make good watchdogs. They can be quick to bark if given a good reason.

Schnauzers like to please their owners. But they can be stubborn, too. Don't let him get away with bad behavior.

You will need to take your new dog to the vet for a checkup. He will need shots, called **vaccinations**, and yearly checkups to keep him healthy. If you think your dog may be sick or hurt, call your vet.

A GOOD FRIEND

Schnauzers are smart, lively, loving, and noisy. Like a good friend, your schnauzer will be quick to protect you. Enjoy your schnauzer for many years.

A healthy schnauzer can live as long as fourteen years.

NOTE TO PARENTS

It is important to consider having your dog spayed or neutered when the dog is young. Spaying and neutering are operations that prevent unwanted puppies and can help improve the overall health of your dog.

It is also a good idea to microchip your dog, in case he or she gets lost. A vet will implant a microchip under the skin containing an identification number that can be scanned at a vet's office or animal shelter. The microchip registry is contacted, and the company uses the ID number to look up your information from a database.

Some towns require licenses for dogs, so be sure to check with your town clerk.

For more information, speak with a vet.

There are many dogs, young and old, waiting to be adopted from animal shelters and rescue groups.

Words to Know

agility competitions Events in which dogs perform different tasks, such as jumping over hurdles and running up and down ramps. The dog with the fastest time and least amount of mistakes wins.

breed A kind of dog.

fetch To go after a toy and bring it back.

groomer A person who bathes and brushes dogs.

leash A chain or strap that attaches to the dog's collar.

shed When a dog's hair falls out so new hair can grow.

vaccinations Shots that dogs need to stay healthy.

veterinarian (vet) A doctor for animals.

Read About Dogs

Books

Brannon, Cecelia H. *Pet Dogs*. New York, NY: Enslow Publishing, 2016.

Carney, Elizabeth. *Woof! 100 Fun Facts About Dogs*. Washington, DC: National Geographic Children's Books, 2017.

Johnson, Jinny. *Miniature Schnauzer*. Mankato, MN: Riverstream Publishing, 2015.

Wilson, Jeanette. *Miniature Schnauzers*. Broomall, PA: Mason Crest, 2018.

Websites

American Canine Association Inc., Kids Corner
www.acakids.com
Visit the official website of the American Canine Association.

National Geographic for Kids, Pet Central
kids.nationalgeographic.com/explore/pet-central
Learn more about dogs and other pets at the official site of the National Geographic Society for Kids.

INDEX